Washington, DC

in 3 Days:

The Definitive Tourist Guide Book That Helps You Travel Smart and Save Time

"Finest City Guides"

Book Description

Washington, DC in 3 Days is your all-in-one guide to up-to-date, important advice on where to stay, where to eat and what to see in your short visit. You could spend the entire three days at the Smithsonian Museums, but of course you'll want to see the other historic sites, so you can choose just a few of the Smithsonian museums to check out – they're all free!

Enjoy and take pause at the memorials and monuments as they are lit at night, and take a shopping break on the cobbled lanes of Georgetown.

Inside this handy guide, you'll find:

- Hotels in several budget ranges
- Restaurants in three budget ranges and covering many cuisines
- Information on the sights you won't want to miss

- Inside tips on using public transit to get around just like the locals do
- Descriptions of the neighborhoods you will be staying in and visiting
- Tips on staying safe in the capitol of the United States

As you read through, make plans on what to visit and where to stay. Get to the physical and symbolic heart of this historic city. Start your journey here!

The People of Washington, DC

To most Americans, Washington, DC is simply the nation's capital. The federal lawmakers from all 50 states sit here and craft the laws and bills that change the country, for better or worse, for all people who call the United States home. But there is so much more here than just the government.

The people of Washington, DC reflect a mid-sized, cosmopolitan, ethnically diverse city. The population was over 672,000 in 2015, which is 100,000 higher than the census taken in 2000.

Washington, DC was not an organic town, but a political compromise. The federal government's presence was instrumental in the development and growth of the city. It's easy to forget, since it's the capital of the country, that Washington also has a population of native residents.

The city had an African-American majority until 2011. At that time, the black population of the city slipped below the 50% mark for the first time since the late 1950s. Some of the neighborhoods in DC are noted for their valuable contributions to black culture and history.

As was the case with many northern cities, Washington experienced an influx of black migrants from the South, in what was known as the Great Migration. They went north for better jobs and education opportunities. They were also escaping black-white segregation, and even lynching.

Language

In 2005, a study showed that over 85% of the residents of Washington, DC speak English as the only language in their homes. Over 8% speak Spanish and just over 1% speak French.

The DC Dialect

Newcomers to the United States are sometimes confused by the "Washington" in Washington DC, since there is also a Washington state. Washington, DC is located in the District of Columbia, which is not a state.

DC loves its acronyms, too. From POTUS (President of the United States) to the agencies, like the FBI, DoD, CIA and NSA, etc., there are so many it seems like you're texting when you're talking.

Holidays

New Year's Day	January 1
Dr. Martin Luther King, Jr. Day	January
President's Day	February
Memorial Day	May
Independence Day	July 4
Labor Day	September
Columbus Day	October
Veterans Day	November
Thanksgiving Day	November
Christmas Day	December 25

Religious Beliefs

Nearly 57% of DC residents state that they are affiliated with a religion. Over 15% are Catholic, 0.10% are Latter Day Saints, and over 7% are members of other Christian faiths. Jews make up over 3% of the population in DC, nearly 2% are members of an Eastern faith and just over 0.50% are Muslim.

Here is a quick preview of what you will learn in this tourist guide:

- Helpful information about Washington, DC
- Flying into the city
- Transportation tips in town
- Why Washington, DC is such a vibrant tourist spot and what you will find most remarkable about it
- Information on luxury and budget accommodations and what you'll get for your money
- The currency used in Washington, DC
- Tourist attractions you should make time to see
- Other attractions for entertainment and culture
- Events that may be running during your stay
- Tips on the best places to eat & drink for all price points, whether you want simple fare, worldwide dishes or US flavor

Table of Contents

Introduction

Visiting the DC area, on the Potomac River, you'll find that it has the perks of any other metropolitan city. It has a very extensive public transit system, and you can find a seemingly endless cumber of entertainment venues, museums, cultural sites and restaurants. You may not always be in the District of Columbia – some of the sights are in the cities and states that geographically abut against DC.

Each neighborhood has a unique atmosphere. From parks to coffee shops, the ambiance is almost like that of a single, smaller community. Washington, DC borders the states of Virginia and Maryland. It is clearly defined by the imposing neoclassical buildings and monuments, including the buildings that are home to the three branches of the US federal government.

A Brief History of Washington, DC

In 1790, the first president of the United States, George Washington, chose this location to be the US capital, specifying the precise spot, along the Anacostia and Potomac Rivers. The vision was modern for its time, including ceremonial spaces and grand boulevards. The city was designed as a grid, with the streets like spokes in a wheel. All the points lead to the Capitol Building.

In 1812, shortly after its establishment, war with Great Britain nearly took DC away. Their army invaded DC and set fire to many of its buildings. The Library of Congress, the White House and the US Capitol Building were burnt to the ground.

In the later 1860s, the city became a hub for slaves freed during the US Civil War. Abolitionist Frederick Douglass became one of the new residents, and there was a steady growth in the African American population.

After the War of 1812 and the 1860s Civil War, the district was expanded when it absorbed Georgetown and a number of other surrounding areas. In the 1900s, downtown neighborhoods were developed. Streetcar lines expanded, which added more energy to the city's growth. In the early years of the 1900s, DC was the first American city to plan urban renewal projects like the "City Beautiful" movement.

In 1968, the leader of the civil rights movement in the US, Dr. Martin Luther King, Jr., was assassinated. Violence erupted in DC, as rioters took to the streets passionately. Numerous buildings were destroyed by set fires. The riots continued for over three days, and they were only stopped when federal troops were brought in.

Travelers come from all over this world to see the scenic views and visit historical sites in Washington, DC. Its memorials, museums and monuments are world-famous, and there is something to interest everyone in DC.

Neighborhoods

As locals will tell you, DC is made up of various neighborhoods, which have nothing to do with the governing of the country. There are no politics in the local neighborhoods, and no powerplays. Each neighborhood is unique, and some have a lot to offer travelers.

We'll highlight the neighborhoods you'll likely be visiting.

Anacostia

Washington DC offers all types of local, international and national experiences. If you're interested in African American US history, hop on the Metro's Green Line, which will take you to Anacostia. This area was once a very high crime district, but since 2015, crime has been steadily on the decline.

Frederick Douglass House

Cedar Hill is a draw for many tourists. It's the former home of Frederick Douglass, and is now a historic site. You can only get inside the home if you take a guided tour. It includes artifacts that once belonged to Douglass, who went from being a slave to an abolitionist. The Anacostia Historic District houses about 500 other buildings.

Capitol Hill

This is a popular place to live. It offers 19th-century rowhouses and a vibrant nightlife and dining scene. Tourists, along with young government staffers, head to this area for its government buildings, including the Supreme Court and the US Capitol. The surrounding area has restaurant-filled, historic blocks.

The US Capitol can be toured through its visitors' center. Guides take small sized groups beneath the intricately painted dome and the Old

Supreme Court Chamber. The tour requires a reservation, as will a visitation to the Senate or Congress, when they're in session.

Downtown

The downtown area of DC is a cosmopolitan neighborhood, offering an eclectic mix of must-see museums, in-demand restaurants and high-end shopping. The most famous address in the city, 1600 Pennsylvania Avenue, is the White House, nestled right on the downtown DC border, which gives the neighborhood a feeling of sophistication and importance.

You may want to take some time in this neighborhood to visit the National Museum for Women in the Arts and the Renwick Gallery of the Smithsonian American Art Museums.

Foggy Bottom

Fog lingers naturally here, in the neighborhood that stretches from the west end of Georgetown to the Potomac River. It holds diplomatic and cultural edifices and is bordered by the West End neighborhood, which boasts many hotels and restaurants.

Many visitors come to visit the John F. Kennedy Center for the Performing Arts. This is a living memorial to this past president. World class drama, music and dance performances are scheduled almost every night, on nine separate stages.

National Mall

The Washington Monument, as it rises majestically toward the sky, is a prime photo stop for tourists. Sadly, the inside of the monument is closed until 2019, for refurbishing of the elevator. It's still a moving sight from the ground.

The history of America is brought to mind also by the Lincoln Memorial and US Capitol Building on the Mall. Exploring the greenspace on the mall, you will see inspiring museums, memorials and monuments.

The National Mall is the most visited national park in the United States. In this area, past, present and future seem closer together than possibly anywhere else. The memorials and monuments here honor American heroes and forefathers who have made the ultimate sacrifice to serve their country. This is also the place where Americans gather to have their voices heard by the elected lawmakers in DC. You may also learn the fragile nature of freedom at the US Holocaust Memorial Museum. If you have time, look into a few of the Smithsonian Museums.

Penn Quarter & Chinatown

This neighborhood boasts Verizon Center, where sports teams, stage theater groups and rock music icons literally take center stage. So, it shouldn't surprise you that there is always something going on here.

Sports fans, shoppers, culture vultures and foodies will all find something they love in these two neighborhoods, located just north of Pennsylvania Ave. NW.

These neighborhoods also are home to the Smithsonian American Art Museum and the Smithsonian National Portrait Gallery. Here, you can study real-life James Bond type spies at the International Spy Museum or pause at the Newseum for a look at the ever-changing journalism world.

Southwest Waterfront

This is among the most historic areas of DC, and that's saying something, in a city steeped in history. Here you'll find the longest continuously-operating open air fish market in the country, along with houseboats and plenty of recreational activities. It also offers easy access to some of the most beloved of DC's memorials and monuments.

The area is also ready to become a hot neighborhood, undergoing revitalization to introduce The Wharf, a new destination on the waterfront, with shopping, dining and water access.

U Street

This area was once the heart of America's black culture. It is also the birthplace of the jazz musician Duke Ellington, a celebrated Washington icon. This section of DC is vibrant, anchored by the lively activity of the 14th Street corridor on the west end and the revitalized Howard Theatre on the east end.

The music and food here are exciting and eclectic. From Ben's Chili Bowl to Italian and soul food, there are so many eateries to experience. The area has been dubbed "Little Ethiopia", with many residents from that African nation. U-Street is both colorful and historic, with some of the city's richest culture, and many boutiques, bars and restaurants.

What does Washington, DC offer its Visitors?

Washington, DC is among the most often visited cities in the United States. It offers many types of experiences, not all of them historic. This vibrant city-district is also the home of great cultural attractions, art and food.

From the myriad of monuments and memorials, a trip to DC offers you a deep look into the past of the United States, the leader of the free world, many believe. The Smithsonian Institution alone holds a myriad of museums – all interesting and all free of charge. You could spend a week in DC easily, but you can still see a lot in three days.

1. Key Information about Washington, DC

Money Matters

Washington, DC, like all cities in the US, uses the US dollar (USD). The most commonly used bills include 100, 50, 20, 10, 5 and 1.

100 cents are equal to $1, and the coins you'll see include 50, 25, 10, 5 and 1 cent.

If you travel on credit or debit cards, there are plenty of banks and ATMs in Washington, DC.

If you're visiting from abroad, you can save fees by using your credit card. Other than street vendors, they are accepted almost anywhere, and you can even charge purchases lower than $1.

When you pay by credit card, they use the current exchange rate, and the high max fee is usually only about one percent.

Tipping

Like all US cities, tipping is very much encouraged in DC, and even expected. You can pay your doorman at the hotel $1 to $2 if he hails a cab for you. If he is carrying your bags, the basic tip is $2 for your first bag and then $1 each for additional bags. They don't need to be tipped if all they do is open the door. Bellhops are usually tipped the same as the doormen.

For maid service, most DC travelers leave between $3 to $5 per day. The maids often change from one day to the next, so you can leave your tip on your pillow to be sure the right person gets it.

Restaurant Tipping

In full service restaurants, where wait staff comes to your table to serve you, the customary tip is between 15 and 20%. Of course, if your service is exceptional, you can leave more.

Transport to and in Washington, DC

Getting to Washington, DC by Plane

The main airport for international travelers in DC is Washington Dulles International Airport. It's over 25 miles from downtown DC. It sprawls over 13,000 acres that straddle the Loudoun and Fairfax county lines. Dulles is just one of three main airports in the DC area, handling over 21 million passengers each year.

Getting to Washington, DC from the Airport

Washington Dulles International Airport offers numerous convenient ways to get to and from the airport. You can get to anywhere on the Metrorail Subway System for less than $11 – just take the Silver Line Express Bus for a non-stop ride from the airport to the Wiehle Avenue Metrorail Station.

The GO Airport Shuttle offers transportation from Dulles International to and from conference centers, hotels, offices and homes in the DC and Baltimore area. You can use sedan services, private van services or the shared ride airport shuttle.

To get to the GO Airport Shuttle at the Dulles Airport, grab your luggage, and head downstairs until you're at ground level. Head to sections 1D and 1E at the curb next to the building. Look for white vans with green GO labels.

Washington, DC Rental Cars

Don't even think about driving in Washington, DC, unless you're bold and daring and ready to fight for parking space. That said, there are plenty of rental car companies at Dulles International. They include Enterprise, Alamo, Avis, Hertz, Thrifty and others.

Washington, DC Airport Cabs

Washington Flyer Taxicabs are routed to serve Washington Dulles International Airport exclusively. They have 24-hour service to and from Dulles.

You do not need to reserve a taxi ahead of time to get to DC. Just follow the Ground Transportation or Taxi signs to the terminal's lower level. Go down the ramp to either Door 2 or Door 6. Customer service representatives are available 24 hours per day.

If you want to take a taxi OTHER than a Washington Flyer, you need to make arrangements in advance with the operators of those taxi companies. Those cab drivers are not allowed to solicit passenger pickup at the airport.

Payment and Tipping for Airport Taxi's

You can pay for your cab with cash or a credit card. Drivers accept MasterCard, Visa, American Express, Diners Club and Discover cards.

You can also pay with an Airline voucher. The service is restricted to the payment terms and destination on the voucher itself. If the amount of fare is larger than the voucher, you are responsible for any difference. Gratuities are at your discretion, and are welcome, and even expected.

Public Transport in Washington, DC

The Washington DC MetroBus includes 325 routes, and 1,500 buses that travel them, helping you to get around more easily. Signs of red, white and blue will identify the bus stations. The fares are inexpensive if you use a SmarTrip Card.

The DC MetroRail is a convenient train system to use for tourists and locals alike. It spans roughly 106 miles and includes 86 stations. The stations are located in many places in DC, marked by brown pillars with a letter M on them. It includes five routes – green, orange, yellow, blue and red, and these may connect with each other in some places.

Passes & Tickets

SmarTrip Cards can be purchased in stored-value form at any Metro station that also allows parking. They are not available at every station, but you can also pick them up through Metro sales offices, using credit card or cash, or on their website, using a credit card.

The cards do have a cost of $5, but you can replace one if it's stolen or lost, as long as you register it. SmarTrip cards are easy to use on buses and rail alike.

DC Taxis

There are many companies that offer taxi service in the Metro DC area – in fact, over 150 companies!

DC taxis are a very convenient way to get from one place to another in the region. They are actually fairly affordable. If you have luggage, a taxi works better than public transit, until you drop your bags at your hotel. Taxis and app companies including Uber and Lyft can pick you up from any point in the city, and deliver you right to your destination.

Taxis are easiest to find on busy streets, in front of main attractions and hotels. They are plentiful outside Union Station and around the National Mall. Hail a taxi as you would anywhere. Take a small step off the curb and hold out your arm. You can call ahead and reserve taxi's, too.

No more than four passengers can ride in sedan-style taxis. One can ride in the front seat, if needed. DC taxis cannot refuse you transport based on your business, disability, political affiliation, sexual orientation, personal appearance, age, sex, national origin, religion, color or race.

DC Taxi Fares

Minimum fare is $3.25.

The mileage charge = $0.27 for each 1/8 mile.

Each additional passenger cost an additional $1.00.

A luggage fee can be charged at $.50 per bag or box placed in the taxi's trunk.

Phone dispatch fee = $2.00.

A $25 per hour surcharge is billed of you leave the driver waiting.

A $15 fee is added during a snow emergency.

Uber - Uber drivers use their own vehicles. Pricing is similar to taxi prices. Payment is taken care of through the Uber app, and not with the driver.

Lyft – This app-based ride transportation can be very affordable by giving you a chance to share your ride. You must arrange rides in advance.

2. Accommodations

There are all kinds of accommodations in and around the DC area. The prices are not cheap overall, but you can go for the lowest on our list and get a reasonably priced hotel that is well within the areas you'd like to sightsee.

Prices for luxury hotels: $500 USD to $900+ USD per night

Park Hyatt Washington
- Close to Ford's Theater, the White House, Washington Monument, Lincoln Memorial

Willard Intercontinental Washington
- Close to Downtown, US Capitol, Washington Monument, Ford's Theater, the White House

The View Apartment Hotel
- Close to US Capitol, Capitol Hill, Smithsonian Castle, Ford's Theater, Washington Monument, Jefferson memorial

Mandarin Oriental, Washington

- Close to US Capitol, Ford's Theater, Washington Monument, Smithsonian Castle, Jefferson Memorial, Capitol Hill

Prices for mid-range hotels: $300 USD to $450 USD per night

Ginosi WaterfrontApartel
- Close to Ford's Theater, United States Capitol, Capitol Hill, Washington Monument, Jefferson Memorial

Hyatt Place DC
- Close to Downtown, Lincoln Memorial, White House, Washington Monument, Ford's Theater

The Watergate Hotel*
Yes, this is the hotel after which the famous Watergate scandal was named
- Close to White House, Lincoln Memorial, Georgetown Waterfront Park

Loews Madison Hotel
- Close to Downtown, Washington Monument, Ford's Theater, Lincoln Memorial, White House

Prices for least expensive hotels: $200 USD per night and less

AC Hotel by Marriott National Harbor

- Close to Market Square Lyceum, Nationals Field, George Washington Masonic National Memorial, Tanger Outlets

Suite Home America DC

- Close to Downtown, Washington Monument, White House, United States Capitol, Ford's Theater, Verizon Center

Found Places Capitol Hill B&B

- Close to Smithsonian Castle, Verizon Center, Ford's Theater, United States Capitol, Supreme Court of the United States, Capitol Hill

The Georgetown House

- Close to Vietnam Veterans Memorial, Lincoln Memorial, White House

Airbnb's

For $40 per night you can stay in a sunny two-room suite with two sleeping areas. It's located right in DC, close to the major attractions and museums. It's also close to Union Station.

$125 per night gets you a fully furnished suite, the Moroccan Room. It's on the second floor of a lovely Victorian Brownstone located in Dupont Circle. This is a very desirable neighborhood for tourists, and also offers fine dining, shops and cafes in the area.

While you're in DC, you could splurge if you like. A cozy private room in historic Capitol Hill is $300 per night. It's within walking distance of the White House, the National Mall, The Smithsonian Museums, the US Capitol and the Library of Congress.

3. Sightseeing

There is so much to see in DC, especially if you're a history buff. From stirring monuments and memorials to the myriad of museums within the Smithsonian Institutions, there is something to interest everyone. You'll also find historic homes where some of the greatest of Americans once lived.

The Washington Monument

** The Washington Monument is closed until spring 2019.

You can still snap some wonderful photos of this majestic monument, but the inside is being restored. It was built to honor the commander in chief of the American Continental Army and the nation's first president, George Washington. It was once the world's tallest building, topping out at more than 555 feet in height.

The White House

Touring the White House is among the most popular things to do when you visit DC. Requests for tickets must be made in advance. It can take up to several months to receive a reservation, but people who have taken the tour say it's very much worth the wait.

If you are not able to get a tour reservation, you can still view the grounds, snap photos from outside and stop at the White House Visitor Center. In this Visitor Center, you can learn more about the history of the White House and the families who have lived there, along with the architecture and furnishings of the first family's home. You can also pick up some souvenirs at the gift shop.

Smithsonian Museums

There certainly won't be time for you to visit all the museums in the Smithsonian Institution, but make time for a few that may interest you. They are wonderful collections of history and science, and they're free! The Smithsonian has 17 museums, multiple galleries, and a National Zoo. There are quite literally millions of art works and artifacts, on display for you to see.

Among the Smithsonian Museums, you'll find:

- National Museum of American History
- National Air and Space Museum
- Smithsonian Museum of Natural History
- National Portrait Gallery
- American Art Museum
- Museum of the American Indian
- African Art Museum
- African American History and Culture Museum
- Anacostia Community Museum

- Steven F. Udvar-Hazy Center
- Freer Gallery of Art
- Arthur M. Sackler Gallery
- Smithsonian National Postal Museum
- Hirshhorn Gallery and Sculpture Garden
- Smithsonian Castle
- National Zoo
- Arts and Industries Building

The National Mall

The Mall is home to some of the most famous museums in DC, and many of the memorials and monuments that make DC such a special place. It's certainly a place you'll want to see.

At one end of the mall is the Washington Monument, and the opposite end will find you at the Lincoln Memorial. Between the two are many pieces of history and architectural masterpieces. Each memorial and monument was crafted as a tribute to the people who helped to shape the United States into the country it is today.

The monuments on the National Mall include:

- Washington Monument
- Vietnam Veterans Memorial
- Jefferson Memorial
- FDR Memorial
- Martin Luther King, Jr. Memorial
- World War II Memorial
- Lincoln Memorial & Reflecting Pool
- Constitution Gardens
- Korean War Memorial

Downtown DC Shopping

Washington DC offers some impressive shopping opportunities, too. The newest area, CityCenterDC, has 10 acres of restaurants, cafes, boutiques, shops and public places. You'll see many global shopping names in CityCenterDC, like BOSS, Burberry, Longchamp, Hermes, Kate Spade and Dior.

Smithsonian's National Zoo

With free admission, this zoo is tough to beat for family fun, or adults keen on learning about conservation. The zoo, since its founding in 1889, has a mission to save habitats and wildlife, to share knowledge and to provided interesting experiences between animals and people. There are two National Zoo campuses. One is a 163-acre urban park in the Northwest portion of DC, and this is the only one open to the public.

4. Eat & Drink

You can find nearly any type of food you like in the streets of DC. With its foreign diplomats and embassies, there are food types from around the world.

Fine Dining Restaurants

The Palm Restaurant - $275 for two

This restaurant has amazing ambience and a very attentive staff. The helpings are generous, and you'll enjoy the various tastes. Some of their favorites include Bone-In Colorado Veal Rib Chop with red onions, shaved fennel, baby arugula and a mozzarella di bufala salad and the Prime Double-Cut New York Strip, sliced tableside, which serves two to three people. Save room for their cheesecake, if you can – it's delectable.

Marcel's - $200 for two

The atmosphere here is quiet, elegant and soft. The service is like it used to be in days gone by. Waiters stand by unobtrusively to clear your plates as you finish them, and bring the next course. Try the lobster bisque, the tender venison or perfectly cooked lamb. The scallops are quite juicy and seasoned perfectly. Either the soufflé or chocolate mousse is wonderful for dessert.

Café Dupont - $150 for two

If you're in DuPont Circle, try this enticing menu. Regulars flock here, with positive experiences every visit. This restaurant is a quiet place to eat, and their wait staff is very friendly and helpful. Among the favorites are salmon, seafood stew in vegetable broth and mussels marinara with fries.

Morrison-Clark Inn - $150 for two

This lovely and historic old inn has a wonderful "feel". The food is consistently highly rated and the service is great. Try the Morrison Clark Burger with brown sugar mustard, pickled red onions, swiss cheese, gingered mushrooms and bacon. Or tempt your taste buds with the Grilled Chicken Club, with garlic aioli, gruyere, tomato, greens and bacon on sourdough bread.

Fiola Mare - $100 for two

Exceptional service and great food bring people back to Fiola Mare for repeat visits. The wine selection is extensive for a smaller sized restaurant. Regulars say there isn't anything on the menu that isn't great, but they do recommend the New Zealand salmon, Black Diamond Mussels and Maine Lobster.

Oval Room - $100 for two

This restaurant is very popular, with good reason. The food is tasty and the service is impeccable. Among the favorites are chilled fresh pea soup, which has rave reviews, and the Butter Roasted Strip with Cippollini onions, Chanterelle mushrooms and potato pava.

Midrange restaurants

Sequoia - $90 for two

This mid-range restaurant has a wonderful location and the ambiance is relaxing. You'll enjoy sitting outside, if the weather permits. Try the lobster and steak, the Chilean Sea Bass or the Prosciutto di Parma, which has a subtle nuttiness, a velvet-smooth texture and a sweet & salty flavor.

Filomena - $85 for two

This restaurant offers authentic Italian taste and large portions. The staff and waiters are friendly and helpful. The ravioli stuffed with beef brisket is delicious, and the veal chops are very popular.

Mango Tree - $85 for two

Entice your taste buds with duck spring rolls, which are delightfully flaky and crispy. This restaurant is also famous for its Butcher's Cut in curry sauce, plated with grape tomatoes and Brussel sprouts in thick, savory curry sauce. You might also like to try their shrimp pad Thai, with tamarind sauce, tofu, bean sprouts, chili and peanuts.

Al Crostino - $80 for two

This establishment offers you a great Italian meal before you head out to a club or other night spot. Their pan-seared New Zealand lamp chops arrive lightly tossed in bread crumbs and fresh herbs, finished with honey balsamic glaze. Another popular choice is cast iron baked eggs, served with bacon, mushrooms and spinach and accompanied by roasted potatoes.

Le Diplomate - $75 for two

You're in for an amazing experience when you visit Le Diplomate. It has the atmosphere of a large French Bistro, and draws an eclectic mix of diners. Among the favorite dishes include duck and tender veal, crème brulee and cheese platters, with single glasses of wine, champagne and port. The veal entrée includes a wonderful multi-flavored sauce.

BlackSalt Fish Market & Restaurant - $75 for two

As you enter this restaurant, it looks more like a fish market. Don't be confused. They do both very well. The restaurant has a justified reputation for great fish, with quality dishes that are beautifully prepared.

Try the butter poached lobster, with lobster-sherry butter, roasted mushrooms, asparagus, fava bean porcini puree and house gnocchi. Or perhaps tempt your taste buds with wood grilled baby octopus with confit gold potatoes, salsa verde and spice peperonata.

Cheap eats

Chinatown Express - $30 for two

This is all you'd expect in a Chinese place and more. The servers do not speak much English, but they still take orders properly. You can start off with rich, thick egg drop soup with perfectly cooked leek dumpling and pan fried pork. Some other favorites include shrimp with mixed vegetables and handmade noodles with stir fry beef.

Tortilla Café - $25 for two

This café is known for fast service and authentic Mexican food. Try their carne asada with grilled steak with jalapenos and sautéed onions or the chicken or beef fajitas with sour cream, guacamole and salsa.

Habesha Restaurant - $25 for two

For authentic African food, this is the place to go. Their Ethiopian dishes are much tastier than the low price would indicate. It's always somewhat crowded, so that tells you a lot about how great their food is. You can split dishes like the meat and vegetable platter – there is plenty of food for two in it. Repeat customers also recommend the spicy potatoes and collard greens.

Bonchon - $20 for two

This Korean restaurant offers great food at a reasonable price. The pot stickers with chicken and rice are popular, as are their chicken sliders. The mains are large enough to share, and the service is excellent. Try their house fried rice, Bulgogi wrap and Bull Dak.

Pita Pit - $25 for two

This small restaurant specializes in Middle Eastern, Greek and American fare. The service is fast and the food is plentiful, but the ambiance is just that of a food court, which is what Pita Pit is. Among their favorite dishes are the Dagwood with prime rib, turkey and ham and the Chicken Caesar with chicken, romaine and bacon.

5. Culture and Entertainment

Washington, DC has a culture influenced by the federal government presence. The government was instrumental in the development of numerous cultural memorials in the city. Washington's U-Street was an important area for African American culture early in the 20th century.

Many national landmarks call DC home, and it is an exceedingly popular tourist destination. The National Mall is a large and open area in the city's center, which features many monuments of American leaders.

Arlington National Cemetery

This may well be the most awe-inspiring sight you will visit in Washington, DC. Here are laid to rest over 250,000 men and women who served in the US military. It is also the home for the Tomb of the Unknown Soldier, who is an unidentified American soldier who fought and died in WWI, and other unknown soldiers from WWII, The

Korean War and the War in Vietnam. This tomb is a very somber place, guarded 24/7, regardless of weather, including heavy rain and blizzards.

You may also be moved by the Eternal Flame, marking the grave of President John F. Kennedy, and a tribute to Robert E. Lee, the Arlington House.

The Lincoln Memorial

The impressive Lincoln Memorial towers above the Reflecting Pool at the west end of the National Mall. The shimmering waters illuminate the structures surrounding it, which honor the most storied leaders in American history.

Stroll slowly toward the Lincoln Memorial from the east, watching it grow larger as you get closer. When you're standing in front of it, gaze at its marble columns, inspired by Greek temples of ancient times. 36 columns mark the number of states in the United States when President Lincoln died. This impressive memorial is nearly 100 feet tall.

National Museum of African American History & Culture

This museum is the only one to devote its space solely to documenting African American culture, life and history. A 2003 Act of Congress established the museum, and it holds 36,000+ artifacts. It is the newest museum in the Smithsonian Institution.

The National Gallery of Art

This wondrous gallery and the attached sculpture garden is a DC national art museum, found on the National Mall. Admission is free, as it is at all Smithsonian museums. The main collection includes pieces of art that have been donated by many Americans. The decorative art, medals, sculpture, photos, prints, drawings and paintings trace Western Art development from the Middle Ages to today, including America's only painting by the famous Leonardo da Vinci.

Washington, DC Night-Life

DC is government-centered and serious during the day, but when the sun sets, the district is transformed into a nighttime playground for tourists and locals alike. You can see a show, dance until all hours of the morning, or relax with a drink and people-watch. The DC area has a club for anyone's favorite type of music.

Black Cat

Many bands like Radiohead and the Foo Fighters have played at the Black Cat since its opening in 1993. It brings the best live indie music to DC. The main concert room is 7,000 square feet, hosting large acts, and the backstage area offers more intimate, smaller experiences with punk, indie and solo artists. They also have DJ's, karaoke and comedy shows.

Nightclub 9:30

The locals call this the 9:30 Club, and many popular bands and musicians play here, in this small venue. While you enjoy the great music, order a yummy dish from the club menu – it includes vegan and vegetarian-friendly dishes as well as the usual club fare. With four bars inside, you're sure to find a place to relax and unwind with spirits or even non-alcoholic beverages. If you need a caffeine boost, check out their coffee bar.

Blues Alley

Stepping into this Georgetown club is like stepping into the famous supper clubs of the 20's and 30's. Blues Alley began in 1965, and many famous artists, like Wynton Marsalis and Dizzy Gillespie, have played in this venue.

While you enjoy the jazz, try their club menu, which includes shrimp & artichoke hearts and baked salmon. This is a listening club, not a raucous club, so you're expected to be respectful while musicians are playing.

6.Special Events in Washington, DC

Dr. Martin Luther King, Jr. Day
January

The nation, including people of all colors, pauses to mark the birthday of Dr. Martin Luther King, Jr., with a day of service. Enjoy the free Kennedy Center concert by the Freedom Choir. There is a wreath-laying ceremony at the African American Civil War Memorial in the U Street area. It's also an excellent day to visit the MLK memorial.

National Cherry Blossom Festival Parade
March/April

If you love parades, visit DC during the National Cherry Blossom Festival. The parade route includes 10 blocks on Constitution Avenue, and includes celebrities, singers, dancers, floats and bands. This event (after the parade) starts in late March and runs through the middle of April, with many cultural events, like the Blossom Kite Festival and the Southwest Waterfront Fireworks.

Tram Tour at the National Arboretum April/May

Another flower-related event – this one allows you to hop on the open-air Tram Tour in the US National Arboretum. It celebrates for two weeks the full bloom of the local azaleas. The US National Arboretum has cultivated and curated the most expansive azalea shrub collection in the country. The celebrations are held in the end of April and in early May, for Mother's Day.

Memorial Day   May

Memorial Day brings Americans to picnics and barbeques, but there is a somber reason for the holiday. The nation honors its fallen U.S. Military heroes this day, those who perished in battle, numbering over one million souls. The ceremonies occur at the WWII Memorial, the Vietnam Memorial and the Korean War Memorial. All these memorials are found on the National Mall.

At Arlington National Cemetery, volunteers hand out roses to veterans, families and guests who have come to pay their thankful respect. The president marks Memorial Day by laying a wreath at the Tomb of the Unknown Soldier and in the afternoon, there is a 21-gun salute performed by naval officers.

Family Days at the Air & Space Museum Monthly

Each month, the museum hosts Family Days at both locations. These events give families a chance to experience each museum with interactions with aviators, hands-on activities and interactive demonstrations.

Citi Open   July

The Rock Creek Tennis Center holds the Citi Open every July. Both emerging and established stars of tennis from all around the world compete. There are various ticket options available.

H Street Festival September

This is a high-energy block party that includes beer tents and live bands, but it is more famous for its many ethnic eateries that are participants in the gathering. In addition, you can purchase DC-themed merchandise from neighborhood artists.

National Christmas Tree Lighting December

The National Park Service holds the National Tree Lighting on the White House grounds each December. They light the tree initially early in December, and then a concert is held. Each night afterward, the tree is lit and there are other performances.

Around the National Tree is the "Pathway of Peace", with trees from each territory and state in the United States, each decorated with hand-made, one of a kind ornaments.

7. Safety in Washington, DC

Washington, DC is the political center of the United States. It used to be a dangerous city, but there has been a sharp decline in crime after a stronger focus on preventing it. DC as a whole is safer, while some areas still have problems.

Downtown DC and the National Mall have a large police presence, and this is a safe place in Washington, DC.

The North Central neighborhood is famous for its vibrant night life, trendiness and cultural diversity. The crime level in this area is lower now than it used to be. However, there is a chance of being mugged in public housing areas or bars. Avoid empty streets and dark alleys.

18th Street in the Adams Morgan neighborhood has seen many incidences of pick pocketing, particularly at the time in the early morning when the bars close.

The area around Columbia Heights still has the highest rate of crime in DC, according to reports by Spotcrime.

Common Sense Advice

The tips for safety in DC are much the same as those in other large cities worldwide.

- Carry a small bag around your shoulder or use a concealed stomach pouch. Don't carry your belongings in a backpack.

- Keep your wallet in a front pocket.

- Use cards where you can – avoid carrying cash.

- Pay attention on terraces or patios of restaurants, and when you withdraw money from an ATM.

- Beware of people who seem to behave in a strange way. They may be trying to divert your attention so they can steal your money or belongings.

- Don't wear expensive jewelry when touring.

- Don't set your wallet or phone on your table at a restaurant.

- If someone tries to grab your bag or purse, let them have it. Don't risk injury.

- Thieves and pickpockets work commonly near the monuments and memorials frequented by tourists, along with subways, airports, train stations, trains, beaches and hotels.

- Most pickpockets work in small groups, but they may work alone, as well.

Conclusion

This up-to-date guide to the capital of the United States shows you recent additions that make your visit even more compelling. These guides are designed to be used both when planning your trip and after you have arrived. This book includes:

- A wide variety of hotels in all price ranges
- The must-see attractions as well as a few others that may interest you
- Events and festivals you may want to schedule your trip to visit
- How to get from Dulles International Airport to downtown DC
- How to use public transit to get around town
- Information and attractions specific to the most popular neighborhoods

You're now ready to book a great hotel and plan your itinerary, so you can get in as much sightseeing as possible during your three-day visit.

17582817R00034

Printed in Great Britain
by Amazon